CATS
of the
WILD

OCELOTS

Henry Randall

PowerKiDS press™

New York

Published in 2011 by The Rosen Publishing Group, Inc.
29 East 21st Street, New York, NY 10010

First Edition

Editor: Joanne Randolph
Book Design: Ashley Burrell

Photo Credits: Cover, pp. 16, 24 (center left) Shutterstock.com; p. 5 Sarabia Photo/Getty Images; p. 6 © www.iStockphoto.com/Andrea Poole; pp. 8–9, 24 (left, right) Jupiterimages/Photos.com/Thinkstock; p. 11 © www.iStockphoto.com/Thomas Polen; p. 12 © www.iStockphoto.com/Shane Partridge; p. 15 © Joe McDonald/age fotostock; p. 19 © BIOS/Montford Thierry/Peter Arnold, Inc; p. 20 Purestock/Getty Images; p. 23 © Rene Frederic/age fotostock; p. 24 (center right) Digital Vision.

Library of Congress Cataloging-in-Publication Data

Randall, Henry, 1972-
 Ocelots / by Henry Randall. — 1st ed.
    p. cm. — (Cats of the wild)
 Includes index.
 ISBN 978-1-4488-2519-6 (library binding) — ISBN 978-1-4488-2623-0 (pbk.) —
 ISBN 978-1-4488-2624-7 (6-pack)
 1. Ocelot—Juvenile literature. I. Title.
 QL737.C23R364 2011
 599.75'2—dc22
                                            2010022366

Manufactured in the United States of America

CPSIA Compliance Information: Batch #WW11PK: For Further Information contact Rosen Publishing, New York, New York at 1-800-237-9932

Contents

Do you see the wild cat in this tree? This cat is an ocelot.

Ocelots live in forests in South America and North America. They live as far north as Texas.

Ocelots have beautiful, **spotted** fur. People used to hunt them for their soft coats.

Ocelots sleep during the day. They come out at night to hunt.

Ocelots count on their eyes and ears to hunt. They eat mostly rodents.

Ocelots have sharp teeth and long **fangs**. Ocelots use their teeth to kill animals.

This ocelot hides in the leafy **rain forest**. When an animal it wants to eat walks by, it will jump on it.

Ocelots are good swimmers. They hunt for fish, **iguanas**, and snakes in the water.

This is a young ocelot. Its mother will take care of it and teach it how to hunt.

There are not many ocelots left in the wild. We need to take care of this beautiful wild cat!

Words to Know

fangs

iguana

rain forest

spotted

Index

Web Sites